Is This Normal?

Girls' questions, answered by the editors of

The Care & Keeping of YOU

★ American Girl®

Published by American Girl Publishing, Inc.

Questions or comments? Call 1-800-845-0005,
visit our Web site at americangirl.com,
or write to Customer Service, American Girl, 8400 Fairway Place, Middleton, WI 53562-0497.

Printed in China

09 10 11 12 13 14 15 LEO 10 9 8 7 6 5 4 3 2 1

All American Girl marks are trademarks of American Girl, LLC.

Editorial Development: Erin Falligant, Michelle Watkins

Design: Chris Lorette David; Art Direction: Chris Lorette David, Kym Abrams Design

Production: Jeannette Bailey, Gretchen Krause, Judith Lary, Julie Kimmell

Illustrations: Norm Bendell

Medical Consultant: Dr. Lia Gaggino, Pediatrician

Special thanks to Kristina Heredia of Blues Hair Studio, Madison, Wisconsin.

Cataloging-in-Publication Data available from Library of Congress.

A Letter to
YOU

More than two million girls have read *The Care & Keeping of You.* Those girls have written us letters about everything from braces and bras to pimples and periods. Some girls worry they're growing up too fast. Other girls worry their bodies are lagging behind and will never catch up.

However you feel about your body, you're sure to find letters in this book from girls who feel the same way you do. Reading the letters may feel like talking with good friends—girls just like you. And we hope our responses will answer some of your own questions about your changing body.

If you have more questions (and you probably will), ask your parents or other adults you trust. Too embarrassed? Read the "7 Tips for Talking with Parents" at the back of this book. Talking about your body is a little like ripping off a Band-Aid. It's a lot less painful if you do it quickly and just get the words out. Each conversation will be easier than the last, and you'll feel that much more confident about the changes ahead.

Your friends at American Girl

Contents

Letters about periods, pubic hair, pads & tampons 73

Confused about your period? Not sure what to expect? These responses to girls' questions may help answer some of your own.

Letters about shaving, sports & sleep 87

Noticing dark hair on your legs? Wondering how to stay fit or get a good night's sleep? Find out how other girls on the go are feeling, too.

Advice about talking with parents . . . 103

Read seven tips that will make it easier to talk with your parents about puberty.

Letters about

hair, skin, eyes, ears & mouth

How do you tame tangles? Convince your parents you're ready for pierced ears or contacts? Smile confidently with braces? Deal with acne, birthmarks, and moles? Read these letters and responses to **stay ahead of the game** when it comes to caring for your body.

Dear American Girl,
My hair is long and very thin. I always get tangles when I get out of bed, which means I have to take a shower, and I don't want to do that every morning.

Tangles

To stop snarls before they start, **wear your hair in a loose braid or ponytail at bedtime.** Tie back your hair with a scrunchie or fabric-covered elastic, which is gentler on hair than a rubber band (even the coated kind). When you brush your hair in the morning, start with the ends and work your way up. Hold a small section of hair with one hand while brushing the ends with the other hand. When you shower, **use a conditioner or a detangling lotion,** which doesn't weigh down thin hair. Some detanglers come in spray form, so you can mist your hair while working through wet tangles with a wide-tooth comb. Get your hair trimmed regularly, and think about a shorter cut. A little less length can mean a lot less time and hassle.

Dear American Girl,
Most of my friends are obsessing over their hair. I don't care that much about my hair, but my mom is always telling me that I should. Am I a normal girl?

Careless

What's normal? Some girls are into sports, and some girls aren't. Some girls are into shopping, and some girls aren't. Your mom probably just wants your hair to be **clean and healthy,** and that doesn't require hours of primping. Wash your hair a few times a week—more often if you have oily hair or are very active. And brush it every morning. If your hair falls onto your face, pull it back with a ponytail holder or headband. **Consider a shorter hairstyle** that's easier to care for. And remember that however you wear your hair, you're just as normal as the next girl. A simple hairstyle leaves you time to focus on other things, which makes you a more interesting girl, too.

Dear American Girl,
I hate my short hair, but my grandma thinks it looks cute. She keeps asking me, "Do you want to get your hair cut some more?" I just don't have the guts to say, "No, I want it to grow long."

Not So Cute

Hairstyles change over time. When your grandma was a girl, short styles might have been the in thing. Let her know that you prefer the longer styles girls are wearing today. If you can't tell her, show her. Look through magazines and point out photos of your favorite hairstyles. Ask your grandma which ones she likes, too. If you involve her in your decision to grow your hair, she may be more supportive. If she keeps encouraging you to cut your hair, say (politely), "No, thanks. I'm happy with my hair the way it is." As long as you take care of your hair, you should be able to decide how to wear it.

Dear American Girl,
I got my bangs cut, and now I think I look really stupid. Help!

Bad Bangs

The good news is, hair grows back. Until then, have fun with your bangs. Sweep them off to the side with a cute clip or bobby pin. Push them off your forehead using a wide headband. And wear them down on your forehead often enough to see if you'll get used to them. After a week or two, you might actually like them. But if your bangs are still driving you bonkers, head back to your stylist. He or she can soften the edges between your bangs and the rest of your hair, plus give you tips for growing them out.

Dear American Girl,
I am a black girl with texturized hair. I get my hair relaxed every seven weeks, and it looks great at first. But after two or three days, it looks horrible. How can I take care of it?

Can't Relax

Relaxing, or chemically straightening, your hair can dry it out and weaken it. To keep your hair healthy, have a professional stylist trim it regularly. Don't color or braid your relaxed hair, which may weaken it even more. In between relaxing treatments, wash your hair every 7 to 10 days using a super-moisturizing shampoo. Towel-dry your hair, and apply a leave-in conditioner.

Once a month, treat your hair to a deep conditioner. Avoid greases and pomades. If you blow-dry your hair, let it air-dry as much as possible first. And steer clear of curling irons and straighteners. Is your hair still hurting? It may be time to take a break from the relaxing treatments. Talk to your stylist to find out how.

Dear American Girl,
Everyone teases me about my blonde hair—even my friends! They make up dumb-blonde jokes and call me a ditz. I sometimes go along with it, but it's getting out of hand.

Not a Dumb Blonde

It's hard to keep laughing on the outside when you're hurting on the inside. **Let your friends know that you're tired of the jokes** and that you're not laughing anymore. Say, "I know you're just kidding around, but joking about my IQ hurts my feelings. Could you please stop?" Remind them that there are plenty of super-smart blondes, and **ask your friends to help you set the stereotype straight.** When other people suggest that blondes aren't so smart, say as casually as you can, "That may be your opinion, but it's not mine." Whatever you do, don't buy into believing that hair color has anything to do with intelligence. It's simply not true.

Advice from Girls

"Do your friends know it hurts your feelings when they tease you? Ask them how they would feel if you made fun of them. Whether it is about your weight, height, or hair color, it hurts!"
—An American girl, age 12

Dear American Girl,
I REALLY want to get my ears pierced. I know I'M responsible enough, but my mom still says I have to wait till I'm 13. What can I do?

Tired of Waiting

Prove to your mom that you're responsible and mature by respecting her decision. Don't keep bringing it up. (Nothing screams "irresponsible and immature" like whining.) Instead, show your mom how much pierced ears will mean to you by starting an earring collection or saving money to put toward the cost of the piercing. Buy some stick-on or clip-on earrings, too, so that you can practice wearing them. When your mom sees how serious and excited you are, she may allow you to pierce your ears early. But if she doesn't, stay focused on the future. When your 13th birthday rolls around, you'll have the money and the earrings ready to go.

Advice from Girls

"I tried begging my mom, but that didn't work. Finally I said, 'I'll make my bed.' I never make my bed. I had to make it for a couple of months before she said yes, but it was worth it."
—An American girl, age 10

Dear American Girl,
I'm probably going to get glasses, and I really don't want to. My mom says I look good in glasses, but I don't!
Dreading Glasses

If you don't like the way you look in glasses, you probably haven't tried on enough styles. There are a ton of fun styles in colors ranging from copper to bubble gum. Some frames are decorated with beads and gems, and others with swirls and stars. There are frames so thin, you can barely tell they're on! Ask your mom if you can visit an eyeglass shop or two, and bring a friend along for another opinion. When you're sporting your new glasses, focus your vision on the people around you. Lots of them will be wearing glasses, and they may be looking back at you, admiring *yours*.

Dear American Girl,
I'm in sixth grade and I wear glasses. I want contacts, but my parents keep saying, "Maybe next prescription." I've been waiting for two years!
Responsible Enough

Are your parents worried about your health and safety? Contacts need to be cleaned and stored properly to prevent eye infections. Show your parents you're up to that task by being responsible about other hygiene habits. Brush and floss your teeth every day. Keep your hair combed. Take showers without being reminded.

If you're into sports, remind your parents that contacts are safer than glasses on the court or field. If your parents still think you're too young, ask them to talk with your eye doctor to get the facts. Then relax, knowing that there's nothing more you can do and that you'll have those contacts one day soon.

Advice from Girls

"If you need to wear glasses, just wear them. Think of your glasses as a cool fashion accessory. That's what I do, and I don't feel embarrassed to wear them anymore."
—An American girl, age 11

Dear American Girl,
I've had sore throats for three years now, and my doctor said I might have to get my tonsils removed. I'm so scared!

Scared of Surgery

It's scary to think about surgery, but tonsillectomies are common. **Ask around**—you may be surprised by how many friends and relatives have had one. The surgery is usually over quickly. You may have to stay at the hospital for four or five hours after surgery, but most kids don't have to stay overnight. Your throat will be sore for a few days to a week, but your throat is sore right now anyway, right? And after surgery, you can have all the ice cream and popsicles you want! Do you have other fears? **Talk with your doctor and your parents about what to expect.** And remember that after you recover, you can kiss most of these sore throats good-bye.

Dear American Girl,
My two front teeth are big and crooked. The teeth right beside them are not fully grown, and they're crooked, too. I have to wait six months before I can get them fixed. I want to look cool—not like a chipmunk!
Chipmunk Teeth

Every girl has some feature that she doesn't like. The good news is that crooked teeth can be fixed. Even before you get braces, your teeth will change a little on their own. Your front teeth will look smaller when the teeth beside them come in more fully. Need proof? Look at the mouths around you. You'll see lots of changes happening as your friends' permanent teeth come in and braces go on and off. Other people are probably more focused on their own teeth than they are on yours. So flash them a big smile, and then forget about your teeth for a while.

Advice from Girls

"I'm sensitive about my front teeth because they're really large. I used to try to hide them because some people made fun of me. I know braces will help someday. Until then, I remind myself that I always look better when I smile."
—An American girl, age 12

Dear American Girl,
I have a big problem. I am getting braces right before school starts. I'm afraid everyone will think I look like a dork!

Can't Face Braces

Most kids will look a little different when school starts up again. Some will be taller. Some will have new hairdos. Some will be sporting pierced ears, and many—like you—will have braces. Braces are so common now that lots of adults are wearing them, even celebrities. Your braces won't be the talk of the school. If you want to take the attention off your mouth on the first day of school, wear a new shirt or a sparkly hair accessory. But remember that your best accessory is your smile. If you smile wide and show off your braces, you won't have to worry about hiding them anymore. And you'll see that they're not the big deal you're making them out to be.

Still worried? Here are some reassuring words from girls like you:

"When I got braces, I was worried, too. But when I went to the first day of school, about half the school had braces! Nobody noticed mine. Just be yourself and don't worry about your teeth."
—age 12

"Braces are cool! You get to change the colors of your bands and eat ice cream or pudding when you have them tightened. I have straight teeth, but I would love to have braces."
—age 13

"Remember this: kids all over America have braces. Next time you have an orthodontist appointment, ask for cool colors for your bands so that you can express yourself."
—age 12

"Don't fret! Tons of other girls in your grade will have braces. If someone hurts your feelings, tell some of the other girls with braces how you feel. They'll understand and be able to relate."
—age 10

"Once my friend came back to school with her braces OFF, and she got a lot of attention. We had to get used to her new look because we all thought braces looked so good on her."
—age 9

Dear American Girl,
I will probably be getting braces, and I've heard some horror stories. One girl in my class got her braces stuck to her cheek. She had to get stitches! How can I feel less nervous?

Nervous Nellie

Talk to other girls with braces to find out what's common and what's not. The more people you talk with, the easier it will be to separate horror stories from hard facts. It's common for teeth to hurt for a week or two after you get braces, and again when you get them tightened. But you'll get used to them, and then they usually won't hurt. It's also common for wires from your braces to poke or irritate your cheek, but they rarely get stuck. Your orthodontist will give you wax to rub over the wires so that your cheeks can glide on by. And when you're sore? You can reach for ice cream and other soothing treats. Lots of girls say that's the best part!

Dear American Girl,
Two of my friends like to have gum, but I can't because I have braces. My mouth waters when they chew gum. How can I tell them that it's not fair to me?
Drooling

Try talking with your friends. Say, "When you chew gum, it really makes me want some, too. Can you save that for when I'm not around?" Your friends might cut back on the gum chewing, or they might not. Either way, it's good to have a backup plan for fighting temptation. Which snacks do your orthodontist and dentist say are O.K. to eat? Have those snacks handy, and pull them out when your friends are chewing on things you can't. Satisfy your cravings with bubble-gum-flavored toothpaste and floss. And think about how your teeth will look when those braces come off. Your smile will be bright and beautiful, and you'll be able to chew all the gum you want.

Dear American Girl,
I have red hair and light skin, and I blush A LOT. One of my friends laughs at me when I blush. I don't like it, but I don't know how to tell her to stop!

Red Hair, Red Face

People's bodies react to stress in lots of different ways. Some people sweat, some people shake, and some—like you—blush. As you know, having someone point out your blushing only makes your cheeks burn that much brighter. The next time your friend laughs at your embarrassment, confront her. Say, "I feel even more embarrassed when you point it out. I wish you wouldn't do that." Let your friend know that the friendliest thing she can do is ignore your flushed face and change the subject. That'll give you a chance to cool your hot cheeks by taking lots of deep breaths or splashing cold water on your face.

Dear American Girl,
I have a birthmark on my face. It gets on my nerves when someone points it out. How can I be proud of it?

Bothered

It's normal for people to be curious about birthmarks. If they comment on yours, **just say, "It's a birthmark. I was born with it."** You can try covering it up with a special concealer from the drugstore, or you can talk with your dermatologist about laser treatments that remove some birthmarks. But by now, you may find it hard to imagine your face without your birthmark. It's part of who you are. Your hairstyle has changed and your body has grown, but **that birthmark has been with you since the day you were born.** That's reason enough to be proud of it.

Advice from Girls

"I have a birthmark on my cheek. Sometimes I want to get rid of it, but I think it makes me special. My grandma says it's there because I was kissed by an angel."
—An American girl, age 10

Dear American Girl,
I have a mole on my face, and hairs grow out of it. Kids at school make fun of it. My doctor says I would need surgery to remove the mole. What should I do?

Mole Woes

Did you know that moles on your face are also called "beauty marks"? Lots of celebrities have them, and some women want beauty marks so badly that they create them using makeup. Yours is natural, so the next time someone teases you about your mole, **take it as a compliment.** Just say, "Hey, thanks!" It's true that you can remove your mole through surgery, but that may leave a white scar. Lots of girls decide to keep their beauty marks instead. If you're bothered by the hairs that grow from your mole, talk to your doctor about ways to safely remove them.

Dear American Girl,
My dad had greasy skin and acne when he was my age, and now I'm getting greasy skin, too. Is there anything I can do to keep my skin from breaking out?

Grease Face

Oily skin isn't a bad thing. Without oil, your face would feel dry and scaly. But as you get older, oil glands may start working over-time. And extra oil can clog your pores and lead to breakouts. Care for your skin before acne starts: Wash your face every morning and night with warm water. Use a mild facial cleanser labeled "oil-free" or *noncomedogenic,* which means it won't clog pores. Follow up with an oil-free face lotion. To fight shine during the day, blot your face with fresh facial tissues. Avoid pore-cleaning strips and toners—they're meant for adult skin. And don't wash your face more than twice a day. If you strip your face of too much oil, your glands will work extra hard to give your skin back the oil it lost.

Dear American Girl,
I had the worst day ever.
I got a zit on the middle
of my nose. My family
says that I need to wash
my face, but I <u>do</u> and the
zit won't come off. Help!

Zapped by a Zit

Scrubbing that zit won't make it go away. Most pimples take a few days to clear up, and scrubbing, squeezing, or picking will only make pimples look more red and swollen. Plus, your fingers may be spreading germs to other parts of your face. To help your zit dry up more quickly, dab it with an acne cream or gel that contains salicylic acid or a low percentage (2.5%) of benzoyl peroxide. Keep acne cream out of your eyes—it's strong stuff and can cause burning. To help prevent new pimples, follow your family's advice: wash your face twice a day with warm water and a mild facial cleanser. But don't beat yourself up if you get another zit. Pimples are common during puberty. If washing your face isn't doing the trick, talk to your doctor or dermatologist about other treatments.

Dear American Girl,
I have pimples, and school photos are coming up! Is there a makeup that covers up pimples but doesn't look like I have it on?

Photo-Phobic

Try a concealer and a sheer or translucent powder. Make sure both are labeled "noncomedogenic." Place a tiny dab of concealer on each pimple, and wait for it to dry. Then lightly apply the powder. Need help? Ask your mom or a friend for a lesson. Practice before picture day, and test your cover-up job by taking a photo of yourself at home. Wash the makeup off your face before you go to bed. When it's time for your actual school photo, look straight at the camera and flash a big smile. You'll look 100 percent better than if you look away, trying to hide your pimples.

Letters about
hands, underarms, breasts & bras

Do you bite your nails? Worry about body odor? Wonder if your breasts are developing normally or if it's time for a bra? Other girls are wondering and worrying, too. Find out how to **break bad habits and trust your growing body.** It's developing at a rate that's just right for you.

Dear American Girl,
I have a very bad habit of chewing my nails.
Whenever my hands aren't doing anything,
I bring them up to my mouth and start biting.
How can I stop?

Nail-Biter

You said it—you chew your nails when your hands don't have enough to do. So **put them to work!** Doodle on a pad of paper, squeeze a stress ball, or play cat's cradle with some string. Keep your mouth busy, too, by chewing on a piece of gum during times when you would normally nibble your nails. Pack nail clippers or an emery board in your backpack so that if you chip a nail, you won't try to "fix it" with your teeth. And **look for ways to reward yourself** when you make it through a day without nibbling. Put a quarter in a piggy bank, and save up for a manicure or new nail polish!

Advice from Girls

"I paint my nails beautifully. Then, when I start to chew on them, I decide they're too pretty to bite."
—An American girl, age 10

Dear American Girl,
I have a bad habit of cracking my knuckles. My friends think it's gross. Do you have any suggestions on how I should stop?

The Crack-Master

Don't tackle this bad habit just because your friends are annoyed by it. You have to want to stop. Otherwise, you probably won't. If you're sure that you're trying to break the habit for the right reasons, ask your friends for help. Make up a secret sign, such as a wink, that they can use to remind you to stop. If they catch you cracking your knuckles, stick your hands in your pockets and count to 60. Then pick up a pencil or rock—any small object—and hold it in your hands to prevent you from starting up again. Set a goal for how long you'll go without cracking. Begin with a minute, and then 15 minutes, and then an hour. When you can go a day without cracking your knuckles, celebrate with your friends!

Advice from Girls

"I cracked my knuckles all the time. Then I decided to make a game out of seeing how many hours I could go without cracking them. Before long, I could go for days without doing it. It really helped!"
—An American girl, age 12

Dear American Girl,
I have a terrible habit of picking the skin off my fingers. I'm afraid they will get infected, and my mom is getting annoyed. What should I do?

Sore Fingers

First, try to keep your hands busy (see page 32 for tips). Second, **keep the skin around your nails moist.** Apply hand lotion every day, and use acetone-free nail polish remover to take off old polish. (Acetone can dry out your nails and skin.) If you get a hangnail, a torn piece of skin near your nail, use nail clippers to trim it right away. **Carry clippers** so that you aren't tempted to pick at the hangnail. Always watch for signs of infection, such as red, raw skin around your nails. If your skin seems irritated, dab on a bit of antibacterial ointment, and steer clear of nail polish. See your doctor if your skin doesn't get better. Then work doubly hard to kick this habit and save your poor, sore skin.

Dear American Girl,
My friends say I stink after gym, so I put on deodorant, but they say I still stink. I have tried different deodorants, but they don't work. Help!
Stinky

Everyone sweats—it's your body's way of keeping you cool during exercise. But when sweat mixes with bacteria, it causes an odor. **Wash your underarms with soap every day and after exercise. Then apply a deodorant with** *antiperspirant,* which cuts down on the amount you sweat. If your deodorant isn't working, ask an adult to help you find one with a higher percentage of aluminum chlorhydrate. (If it irritates your skin, stop using it and go back to a lower percentage.) **Wear clean cotton clothes for gym class,** and take them home afterward to wash. If you don't have time to shower after gym, wash your underarms with damp wipes, and reapply deodorant. Are your friends still holding their noses? Then it's time to ask yourself whether these are true friends. Are they pointing out your body odor to help you or to hurt you? Another friend or adult you trust can help you sniff out the difference.

Dear American Girl,
I love my best friend. She is so cool and nice, and she is so fun to be around. The only problem is that she stinks really bad. How can I talk to her about it?

Can't Find the Words

Your friend may not realize that she has to bathe more frequently now that she's getting older. But she's lucky. With support from you, she can resolve the odor issue before other kids start to tease her about it. How can you give her the hint without hurting her feelings? **Try, "I'm worried that I have body odor. Do you worry about it, too?"** Invite her to go shopping with you for deodorant and fresh-scented body washes. If that doesn't work, ask a school nurse or counselor to find a private way to bring up the issue with your friend.

Dear American Girl,
I read about the five stages of breast develop-
ment, and I think I skipped stages 1 and 2.
Is this something to worry about?
Concerned

Nope, you don't need to worry. First of all, you didn't skip stage 1. That's where you started, before puberty began. And your breasts may not look exactly like the pictures you see of the other four stages. Some girls skip one of the middle stages, especially stage 4. And some girls find that one breast grows more quickly than the other, at least for a while. Now that you're watching your breasts more carefully, you may find it easier to track your development through the stages. But no matter what you see in the mirror, don't panic. Your body knows what it's doing. **Breast development is a little different for every girl,** and your body is developing in the way that's right for you.

Stage 1

Stage 2

Stage 3

Stage 4

Stage 5

Think you missed a stage?
Don't panic. Some girls
skip over one of the
middle stages of breast
development.

Dear American Girl,
I share a room with my little sister, and our door doesn't have a lock. Sometimes when I'm changing, she walks right in. I don't want to shut her out of my life. I just want privacy!
Exposed

It's normal for you to want and need more privacy as you get older. To get that privacy, set a new rule for your room: when the door is closed, no one enters without knocking. That goes for you, too, when your sister's inside. Respecting her privacy will make her feel more grown-up and more likely to respect your needs. Pull out your craft supplies so that the two of you can make a "please knock" sign. Post it on the door. If your sister is blowing past the sign, make a game out of it. Teach her a few knock-knock jokes. The time it takes her to tell the joke will give you the time you need to get dressed before she steps inside.

Dear American Girl,
I am starting to get breast buds, and my little sister calls me embarrassing names. When I tell her it's going to happen to her, too, she just laughs. Any advice?
Annoyed

You can look your sister in the eye and say sternly, "Grow up." But the truth is, she already wishes she were more grown-up. She's probably feeling left out, and teasing you is the only way she knows how to stay connected. In a few years, she'll be turning to you for advice about her changing body. Remember that, and try your best to set a good example for her now.

Don't get rattled by the names she calls you. Show her by your calm, confident reaction that a changing body is nothing to be embarrassed about. And give her new ways to connect with you, such as a half hour a day that you set aside for "sister time." If you **give her the attention she's craving,** she won't need to tease you anymore to get it.

Dear American Girl,
My mom says I'm getting breasts, and I don't know how to feel about it. Should I be happy or scared? I'm only nine, and I feel like I'm growing up too fast!
Confused

Most girls entering puberty feel happy and scared. **Ask your mom how she felt** when she started developing breasts. Chances are, she felt some of the same emotions that you do. Remember that breast development is just the beginning of a process that takes many years. You won't wake up tomorrow and be grown up. And **you don't have to suddenly act grown up just because your body is changing.** You can still be a kid. You can still do the things you used to do. The best part is, you might also be able to do things you couldn't do a year or two ago. Can you stay up later? Earn more allowance? Focus on the good parts of growing up. There are many more to come, in time.

Dear American Girl,
I'm always worrying about why my breasts don't grow. Every other girl in my grade has already developed, and I'm still a "youngster." I feel so embarrassed. Help!
The Flat One

It's tough to feel as if you're lagging behind when it comes to development. Lots of girls feel the way you do, and just as many girls worry because their breasts are growing too *fast*. How quickly you develop has to do with your genetics and weight. Some girls don't start developing until they're 12 or 13, but once they start, they often catch up quickly. Check with your doctor to find out where you are on the development path. Then remind yourself that you're normal and you won't be behind forever. Walk tall and show the world that there's a lot more to maturity than the size of your breasts.

Dear American Girl,
The popular girls at school are making fun of me just because my breasts are developing. What should I do?

Picked On

People who make fun of other people are usually trying to make themselves feel better. These girls are probably wishing their breasts were developing, too. That doesn't make the teasing O.K., but it may help you hold your head high and not let them get to you. The spotlight will shift as other girls start to develop. Until then, try this: When someone makes fun of you, don't act embarrassed and scurry away. You have no reason to feel ashamed. Instead, act bored by all the attention. If that doesn't work, look the teaser in the eye. Let her know that what she's saying or doing is harassment. Tell her that you'll let it go this time but that next time, you'll get a teacher involved. And follow through on that promise. You have a right to feel safe and comfortable at school, and other girls do, too.

Dear American Girl,
I have big boobs for being only ten. Boys look at my bra straps when I try to talk to them.
Uncomfortable

Boys your age are curious about girls' changing bodies, and they're not always very good at hiding it. If you notice a boy staring at your chest, tilt your head and try to catch his eye. If he looks away, embarrassed, that's great—you've taught him a lesson about respect. If he doesn't look away or if he seems to enjoy embarrassing you, that's harassment. Let him know that what he's doing is insulting. If the teasing doesn't stop or if you EVER feel scared, talk to a parent, teacher, or school counselor.

What's sexual harassment?
- making sexual comments or comments about your body
- whistling or making rude gestures
- rubbing up against you
- touching, grabbing, or poking your breasts or other parts of your body

Sexual harassment at school is against the law. The school needs to take action to protect you.

Dear American Girl,
I'm going into sixth grade, and every girl but me wears a bra. I feel really left out, but I'm afraid to ask my mom because she might say no. What should I do?
The Only One

Ask your mom if you can **start with a training bra or a sports bra,** both of which are made to fit every size girl. Say, "I'd really like to get used to wearing a bra," or "I'd feel more comfortable wearing one." Offer to save your own money for a bra. If your mom still doesn't think you're ready, remember this: bras are private matters. You can't always tell if a girl is wearing one, which means that other people can't tell that you're not—especially if you layer your shirts. Until you can wear a bra, **try wearing a tank top or camisole** with another shirt over the top.

Dear American Girl,
I need a bra, but I'm an only child and I don't have a mom. How can I talk to my dad without feeling embarrassed?
Speechless

It must be very hard to go through changes like this without a mom, but give your dad a chance. He may be waiting for you to ask him about a bra, and he'll be relieved when you do. You can write him a note. You can open a sales flyer to the bra section and slide it under his cereal bowl. Or you can take a deep breath and say, "Dad, this is hard to talk about, but I think I'm ready for a bra." You'll feel better after the words come out. He will, too. If the thought of going bra-shopping with your dad horrifies you, put your heads together to think of a woman who can take you. Or head to a department store, where a sales associate can help. Either way, you'll have included your dad in something pretty special, and that'll make it easier to talk with him in the future.

It's hard to be one of the first girls to wear a bra. Other girls are bound to be curious and make comments, not knowing how that kind of attention makes you feel. You can head to the bathroom stall to change, but chances are, that'll just draw more attention to you. It may be better to stand your ground. **Change quickly and act confident,** even if you aren't feeling that way. If someone asks you about your bra, simply say, "Yep, I feel more comfortable this way," or "I like bras better than tank tops." Then turn away and get back to what you were doing. Show other girls that your bra just isn't a big deal, and it won't be. They'll take their cue from you.

Dear American Girl,
I HATE wearing bras! They are so itchy. My grandmother says I need to wear one. Can you help me change my mind about bras?
Bra Hater

Bras do take some getting used to, but the good news is that **they come in lots of different fabrics and styles.** Yours may not be a good fit for you. Ask your grandma if you can go shopping for a more comfortable style. Try a soft-cup bra, which is more flexible than an underwire bra. Or look for a bra made of spandex, a stretchy material that moves and bends with your body. Ask a sales associate at the store to bring you the styles that she thinks are the most comfortable, and **keep trying them on until you find one that feels good.**

Dear American Girl,
I'm only in fifth grade and I already wear a B cup bra. My school uniform is see-through, and my bra shows right through. Help!
Can't Cover Up

Try wearing a bra that matches your skin tone. If you can still see the bra through your uniform, layer a tank top or camisole over the bra. Some tank tops have breast support built in, so you can skip your bra and get a smooth look beneath your shirt. If the wires or seams of your bra are showing through your clothing, you may want to shop for a seamless bra or a sports bra. Or consider getting a bigger uniform. The tighter your uniform, the more likely it is to show off every stitch, hook, and wire.

Dear American Girl,
My friend is going through puberty and she doesn't even notice! She wears shirts that her breasts show through because she doesn't wear bras. Some of the boys are starting to notice it, and I am afraid to tell her. What should I do?
Concerned Friend

You should tell her, because if you don't, someone else will—and it'll be easier for her to hear it coming from you. Try something such as, "Have you ever thought about wearing a bra? You could wear a bunch of different styles." Better yet, if bra-shopping is in your near future, invite her to come with you. If you're positive and excited about the experience, she may be, too.

Letters about body image & nutrition

Think you're too short? Too tall? Too thin or too heavy? You're not alone. Lots of girls wish they could change something about themselves. Read letters from some of those girls, and **learn how to care for the beautiful body you call your own.**

Dear American Girl,
I am so short. I am ten years old and I'm only four and a half feet tall. People tell me that height doesn't matter, but that doesn't help!
Shorty

How tall were your parents at your age? Some girls hit their growth spurt later than others. If your parents were "late bloomers," you may be, too, but that doesn't mean you'll be short as an adult. And your friends are right—height has nothing to do with how popular or successful or happy you'll be. If you need more reassurance, seek out other petite girls and women. Ask them to help you make a l-o-n-g list of the advantages to being short. Keep adding to the list, and read it whenever you want a reason to smile about your size.

Dear American Girl,
I am ten years old and I'm really tall. All my friends are shorter. Everyone is always saying, "You're so tall," and it just makes me feel worse.

Stretch

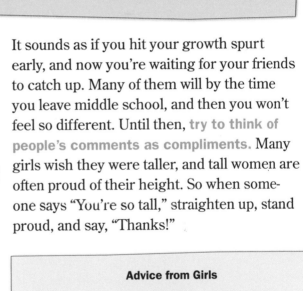

It sounds as if you hit your growth spurt early, and now you're waiting for your friends to catch up. Many of them will by the time you leave middle school, and then you won't feel so different. Until then, try to think of people's comments as compliments. Many girls wish they were taller, and tall women are often proud of their height. So when someone says "You're so tall," straighten up, stand proud, and say, "Thanks!"

Advice from Girls

"If you're really tall (like I am) and people tease or bug you about it, say to them, 'I'm tall? I never noticed.' They'll stop bothering you."
—An American girl, age 10

First, **check with your doctor to find out if you're at a healthy weight** for your age, height, and body type. If your doctor says your weight is O.K., be patient. Girls naturally gain weight during puberty, so you'll most likely fill out as you grow. But if your parents are thin, you may follow in their footsteps. The basic shape of your body is something you're born with, and you shouldn't try to be something you're not. **Focus on keeping your body healthy.** Get involved in sports or other activities that'll make you look and feel strong, not skinny.

Advice from Girls

"If you have a problem with your appearance, remember that your body is still growing and developing. You might like what you see in the years to come."
—An American girl, age 12

Dear American Girl,
I'm concerned about my weight. I'm only ten and I already weigh over 100 pounds. Is this bad? Please tell me the truth.

100-Pounder

If you're like most girls your age, you've gone through a "weight spurt." Many girls gain weight rapidly during puberty, sometimes ten or more pounds in a year. This is normal—you're supposed to gain weight during puberty. While this is happening, don't get too hung up on the number on the scale. Check with your doctor to find out if you're at a healthy weight for your age and height. If your doctor says your weight is O.K., trust that your body knows what it's doing and that your weight will even out as you grow taller.

Dear American Girl,
When I go to the beach, I see girls who are skinnier and prettier than me. I'm not skinny at all, even though I eat right and exercise. I'm afraid I'll never look pretty. Is there anything I can do?
Never Been Skinny

Every girl can look around and spot someone who she thinks is prettier or skinnier than she is. But here's a big truth: skinny doesn't equal pretty. Think of a girl or woman you know who doesn't fit the "skinny mold" but who you think is beautiful. See? There's no one right way to look. Some girls are tall and thin. Some are curvy. Some are strong and athletic. All body types can be beautiful. It's great that you treat your body well by eating right and exercising. Now work on your spirit, too. Take a break from the beach. Surround yourself with girls of all shapes and sizes who are happy with their bodies and aren't trying to look like someone else. You'll find yourself feeling happier and more confident, too.

Dear American Girl,
I'm overweight. I'm a tomboy, and I have a lot of friends who are boys. They don't make fun of my weight right now. But what if when I start to "like" boys, they don't like me because of how I look?
Scared of the Future

The boys you end up "liking" will probably be the same kind of boys you're hanging around right now. That's a good thing, because these are boys who like you for who you are—a fun, athletic, and down-to-earth girl. Some boys do get hung up on looks, but lots of other boys think a good personality and a good sense of humor are more important. You've already got those things going for you. And you know how to be yourself around boys, which will give you a huge head start when you're ready to date.

Dear American Girl,
Friends say I look pretty, but when I look in the mirror, I look really ugly and fat. How do I make myself like what I see in the mirror?
Not the Fairest One of All

Sometimes girls get so used to seeing super-skinny models in advertisements that they lose sight of what's normal and healthy. Girls may see themselves as overweight when they're really not. You're lucky to have friends who see you as the beautiful girl you are. **Spend more time with those friends than you do staring in the mirror.** When you do catch sight of your reflection, pretend that you're looking at your best friend. **Give her a warm smile and pay her a compliment.** Then step away from the mirror. If you still find yourself too focused on the way you look—or if the way you see yourself is starting to affect the way you eat—it's time to reach out for help. Turn to pages 70 and 71 to read more.

Advice from Girls

"Think of yourself as a rare animal. You're the very last one, so try to keep your body healthy."
—An American girl, age 9

Dear American Girl,
It seems like I have to eat every minute. If I stop eating before I'm full, I get hungry again right away. It never feels as if food really fills me up. What should I do?

Hungry as a Horse

It's normal to feel hungry when you're growing, and during puberty, you're growing a lot. **Fill up on snacks rich in protein,** such as whole-wheat toast with peanut butter or hard-boiled eggs. Grab yogurt or a cheese stick. Snack on fruits, vegetables, and whole grains, too, which have fiber to fill you up. And make sure you aren't confusing hunger with thirst. **Drink at least five 8-ounce glasses of water a day.** Still not satisfied? Listen to your body. Is your stomach gurgling? Your mouth watering? If not, you may be confusing physical hunger with boredom, loneliness, or anxiety. **Feed your spirit** by talking with a friend or journaling. Dance to a song or take a quick walk around the block. If you still feel hungry afterward, head to the kitchen for a healthy snack.

Dear American Girl,
I want to eat more fruits and vegetables, but when I eat lettuce and beans, I feel sick. Carrots are O.K., but they're not satisfying. How can I eat healthy foods when I don't really like them?
Forcing It Down

Try mixing healthy foods with foods that you love. Blend fruit with yogurt and skim milk to make a sweet smoothie. Dip carrots and celery into peanut butter or hummus. Both dips contain protein, which not only adds flavor but also helps to fill you up. And talk with your parents about ways to sneak veggies into foods you enjoy. Can you bake them into breads or muffins? Layer them under the cheese on a pizza? Simmer them in spaghetti sauce? Get creative, but don't force yourself to eat anything you really don't like. There are too many good-tasting healthy foods out there to get hung up on the ones that turn your stomach. If you haven't found those yummy foods yet, keep looking!

Dear American Girl,
I can't stop eating junk food. I set a goal not to eat too much, but whenever I see my brother eat it, I get tempted!
Jumpy for Junk Food

Everyone eats *junk food,* or food with little nutritional value, now and then. But it's great that you want to cut back. **Ask your parents to help you** by keeping less junk food in the house. Instead of eating out of the big bag or box, pack single servings into small containers. And substitute healthier snacks when you can. If your brother is munching on chips, reach for almonds. If he's eating candy, grab a handful of raisins. If he's loading up on French fries, dish up a small bowl of hot popcorn. If you're still craving junk food when you're done, let yourself have some of what your brother's eating. But don't be surprised if your cravings are gone—and if your brother's hand is reaching for your bowl.

Dear American Girl,
I eat when I'm watching TV, and most of the time, it's junk food. I feel bad about it, but I can't stop!
Time for a Change

If you eat while you're distracted, you won't really enjoy the food you're eating. You'll also probably eat more than you need—especially junk food. Instead of snacking while you watch TV, pet your dog or bead a bracelet. Keep your hands busy. And **understand the effect that TV ads have on you.**

If an ad comes on for junk food and you start drooling, flip the channel. Or get up and do something active until the commercial ends. Better yet, **turn the TV off altogether** and do something that keeps your mind and your body entertained.

Dear American Girl,
Sometimes my friends forget that I'm a vegetarian. This makes it awkward when I go to dinner at one of their houses. They feel bad when they eat meat around me. How can I remind my friends that I don't eat meat but that it's O.K. if they do?

Veggie Lover

Remind your friends that you're a vegetarian before you go to their house for a meal. Ask if they'd like you to bring your own main course—or pack a peanut butter sandwich, just in case. If they offer you something with meat, politely skip that dish. Don't turn up your nose or say "Eww!" Just say as sincerely as you can, "That looks good," and then pass the dish to the next person. Fill up with an extra helping of salad. If you don't make a big deal out of what you do and don't eat, your friends won't either.

Dear American Girl,
I have a peanut allergy, and I get hives when I eat peanuts. I feel as if my allergy is taking over what I eat!
Can't Eat Peanuts

You're not alone. More than three million kids in America have food allergies. You've probably gotten smart about reading labels and carrying your medication with you. Now get creative about the things you can eat. Instead of a PB&J, try a CC&J (cream cheese and jelly) sandwich. Spread crackers with hummus instead of peanut butter. Ask your parents to help you bake your own cookies and brownies, and always carry a safe snack with you. Visit health food stores, too, which may have special versions of your favorite foods made without peanuts. Want more support from friends? Teach them which foods you can't eat and what an allergic reaction looks like. Better yet, educate your whole class by tackling peanut allergies as a science project. Show them, and yourself, that you control your allergy—it doesn't control you.

Dear American Girl,
I'm a bit of a picky eater. I'm nervous that if I go to a friend's house or restaurant I've never been to before, there might not be anything that I like.
Too Picky

You can check out restaurant menus online or call ahead to see if there's something you like. And your parents may be willing to call your friends' parents to make sure they're serving foods that you can stomach. But you can also **try to be more adventurous in your own kitchen.** Go with your parents to the grocery store, and challenge yourself to choose something new each week. Help to prepare the foods, and try a few bites. You're bound to like some foods that you were pretty sure you wouldn't, which may make you feel braver about trying things at a friend's house. If you don't like something your friend's parents serve, don't make a big deal out of it. **Have another serving of something you do like.** And remember that your tastes will change with time. There will be fewer foods that you haven't tried and many more that you love.

You've already learned a valuable lesson—most weight-loss diets don't work. If you cut down too much on what you eat, you'll end up hungry and may eat more than you would have eaten otherwise. Or your body will worry that it's starving and will try to protect itself. Your metabolism will slow down, which means your body won't use the calories in food as quickly and might store them as fat. Dieting is especially dangerous during puberty, when your body needs extra energy from food to help you grow. Sound complicated? It is. No girl should diet on her own. Check with your doctor first to find out if you are in a healthy weight range. If your doctor says you're too heavy, work together to set up a healthy eating and exercise plan.

Dear American Girl,
My best friend hardly eats anymore. At restaurants, she just orders a diet soda. At her house, she doesn't eat nearly as much as she used to. She always says that she weighs too much, but she doesn't. I'm worried that she might have an eating disorder.
Fearful Friend

You're right to worry. **Eating disorders such as anorexia and bulimia can be very dangerous.** A person with *anorexia* eats very small amounts of food and thinks she's overweight when she isn't. A person with *bulimia* may overeat and then try to make up for it by throwing up. If your friend is still at a healthy weight, she may be in the early stages of an eating disorder, or there may be something else going on. Tell an adult about your fears. **Talk to your parents, a teacher, or a school counselor who can check things out with your friend.** If your friend finds out that you told someone, she may be upset with you, but be patient. In time, she'll see that speaking up was your way of showing her just how much you care.

Sound Like You?

If you think you might have anorexia or bulimia, don't try to deal with it all by yourself. Talk to an adult you trust—a parent, a teacher, a school counselor, or a doctor. Eating disorders can quickly take control of your life. The best way to fight back is to reach out for help.

Letters about
periods, pubic hair, pads & tampons

Do you wonder whether you'll be ready when your period comes? Or how to tell your parents and your friends when it does? Girls have big questions about their periods, and we've answered many of them here. Flip to the back of the book to find out how to ask any other questions that you may have.

Dear American Girl,
I have pubic hair, and I love swimming. How can I wear a swimsuit without hair sticking out?
Longing to Swim

Your swimsuit bottoms should hide most of your pubic hair. If some of your hair sticks out, **try wearing a "boy-cut" suit or a "hipster."** These suits are cut low across the thigh, so they hide hair better than bikini bottoms. As you get older, your pubic hair may spread to the edge of your thighs. Some women shave the edges of their pubic hair, but it's tricky business. Skin in this area is sensitive, and you can end up with painful ingrown hairs. Never shave your bikini area without talking to a parent first.

Dear American Girl,
I'm really worried that when I shower in gym, other girls will notice hair in my private places. What do I do?

Scared About Hair

It's normal to feel self-conscious about your changing body. But these girls you've grown up with are changing, too, and they're feeling just as self-conscious as you are. When you shower, don't waste time looking around to see if other girls are looking at you. They're more worried about their own bodies than they are about yours. Get your shower over with quickly, and then walk—don't run —to your towel. Act confident, even if you aren't feeling that way. You'll show other girls that a changing body is nothing to be ashamed of, and you'll help them feel more comfortable about their own.

Dear American Girl,
My friend and I are at the stage when we could start our periods at any minute. What can we do to help be ready? Is there a way to know when our periods will start?
Want to Be Ready

Once you begin menstruating regularly, you'll be able to tell when your period's coming. Your breasts may be tender, and you may feel cramps in your abdomen and back. You may not feel those warning symptoms the first time you get your period, but you can still prepare for it. Practice wearing a pad so that you can see how it feels. Put together a "first period kit" for school that includes a couple of pads, a change of underwear, and wet wipes, and store the supplies in a makeup bag or a clean, new pencil pouch. Your teacher may have backup supplies for you, too. What's your best defense against a surprise period? Your friend. Make a pact that you'll be there for each other, no matter who gets her period first.

Dear American Girl,
I am 11 years old and about to start my period. My parents are divorced and I live with my dad. I'm scared to ask him for things like pads and tampons. What should I do?

Needing Supplies

You may feel more comfortable buying supplies when you visit your mom or borrowing a few supplies from a friend. But chances are, your dad is already thinking about this and is waiting for you to bring it up. **You can write him a note,** if it's easier. Let him know exactly what you need. **Or just add items to the grocery list**—thin pads with wings, slim-fit tampons with plastic applicators, and so on. The list may lead to a conversation about other ways your dad can support you when you get your period. Being open with him is a great way to let him know that you love and trust him. And **talking with your dad now will make it easier to share other things with him in the future.**

Dear American Girl,
My two best friends have reached puberty before me, and sometimes they'll ask me a question and then will say (nicely), "Oh, wait, you haven't reached puberty yet."
I feel left out, but I don't want to lose my two best friends.
Left Behind

It's painful to feel left out because your friends' bodies are developing more quickly than yours. But there's a lot you can do to bridge that gap. When your friends bring up the fact that you haven't reached puberty yet, **say, "Nope, I haven't, but I will soon. What's it like?"** Ask them questions that show you're interested in what's happening with them. You should be, because you're next! Your friends will appreciate the chance to talk, and you'll feel as if you're still a part of the group. And when your body does start to change, you'll be ahead—not behind. You'll have the benefit of knowing from your friends just what to expect.

Dear American Girl,
My friend got her period. I haven't gotten mine, and I'm a year older! I'm feeling left out. I think that I should mature faster than her. Shouldn't I?
Maturity Mishap

Just as a younger girl can be taller than an older girl, a younger girl can start menstruating first, too. Everyone goes through puberty at her own rate. You can't speed it up or slow it down. And although it's hard when you feel as if you're lagging behind, it's just as hard for girls who go first. Your friend may be scared and a little lonely. Don't let your feelings prevent you from supporting her. Ask her about what she's going through. Admit that you think she's lucky to be maturing in this way. Saying the words may help your envy fade away, and you might learn that your friend envies you because you don't have to deal with menstruation yet. She can help you see the benefits of being right where you are.

Advice from Girls

"Don't think that you can't be friends anymore. When I talked to my friend about how I was feeling, she was glad I did, and we're still friends today."
—An American Girl, age 14

Dear American Girl,
I'm one of maybe three girls in my grade to start her period. I want to tell my friends. But how can I tell them without making it a big deal?
Tell How?

You don't have to share your news with everybody, but it may help you to **talk with a couple of friends you trust.** Break the news as casually as you can. Say, "Hey, guess what? I got my period the other day." They'll have a lot of questions for you, which you can answer—or not—depending on how much you want to share. And who knows? You may find out that one of your friends got her period, too, but was afraid to bring it up. Be open about what your body's going through, and **you'll help your friends to do the same.**

Dear American Girl,
I just started my period, and hardly any blood is showing up at all. Is that natural?
Spotty

Yup, that's natural. **The amount of blood you lose each month is small,** only about four to six tablespoons. Your first few periods may be even lighter than that. You might find a dry stain in your pad rather than actual liquid. And the blood may come and go—a little bit today, nothing tomorrow, and more the next day. Enjoy those light periods while they last. They're perfectly normal, and they're easier to take care of than the heavy ones.

Dear American Girl,
Whenever I get my period, I worry that other people can smell the blood. Can they? How can I stop worrying about it?
Smelly

If you **change your pad or tampon regularly**—every two to four hours—people shouldn't be able to smell the blood. **Bathe or shower every day that you have your period,** making sure to wash well between your legs. If you're still concerned about odor, you can try scented pads. They have perfumes that fight odor, but those perfumes can also irritate your skin. Talk to a parent before using them, and make sure to stop using the pads if you notice any redness or itching.

Dear American Girl,
I get cramps before, after, and during my period. They really hurt, and at school, I don't have any medicine. What can I do to make it better?
All Cramped Up

Pain medicines such as ibuprofen can help ease cramps, but talk with a parent and your doctor to find the right dose for you. Pain medication often wears off after six hours, so some girls keep a bottle at the nurse's office at school. What else helps with period pain? A hot bath before or after school, and staying active during the day. You may feel like sitting out of P.E., but moving your body can ease painful cramps. Keep trying different things. Over time, you'll learn what makes your body feel better, and you'll see that your period doesn't have to "cramp" your style.

Dear American Girl,
I am afraid that my pad will fall out of my underwear when I am changing for gym class. This girl who teases me dresses right next to me! I don't want to use a tampon, though. What should I do?
Dreading the Day

Try a thin pad with wings that wrap around the edges of your underwear to keep the pad in place. **And wear white underwear.** A white pad on white underwear is difficult to see. If your pad does fall out and the girl next to you spots it, take charge. Pick it up and say, "Well, that's embarrassing." Hold your head high and act unconcerned. Your body language will tell her that the moment's passed and you're over it. **Change your clothes, and change the subject.** Start up a conversation with someone else. If you're really nervous or you think your pad may be bloody, duck into the bathroom stall to change it. But don't waste a lot of time hiding. Remind yourself —and this girl—that pads and periods are a normal part of life.

Dear American Girl,
When I try to put in a tampon, it hurts.
Do you have any advice?
Still Trying

A little discomfort is normal, especially if your vagina is dry or you're having trouble relaxing. Make sure to use the smallest-size tampon, one labeled "slim-fit," "junior," or "slender." Look for plastic applicators with round tips, which are easier to insert than cardboard ones. To help an applicator slide in, ask a parent if you can add a little lubricant to the tip of the applicator. Then use a hand mirror to locate the opening to your vagina. As you insert the applicator, relax your muscles. Breathe out as if you're blowing up a balloon. If you feel pain, don't force the tampon to go in. Remove it and try again later. Just keep practicing. You may be able to insert the applicator a little further each time. If not or if you still feel pain, talk to a parent or to your doctor.

Letters about shaving, sports & sleep

Noticing dark hair on your legs? Wondering how to put your best foot forward in sports or in gym class? Having trouble getting a good night's sleep at the end of an active day? **Find out how other girls on the go are feeling.** Learn the facts about fitness and how to put your sleep woes to rest.

Dear American Girl,
I've been getting these long, dark, ugly black hairs on my legs. I've tried to solve my problem by wearing pants, but it's way too hot for pants in the summer. Should I shave or not?
Hairy and Hot

Dear American Girl,
I want to shave my legs, but I'm afraid my mom will say no. I don't really have a good reason for shaving, except I'm really self-conscious about the hair on my legs.
Ready to Shave

Dark hairs on your legs are normal. Other girls your age are sprouting them, too. But if you're too embarrassed by the hair to wear shorts, it's time to invest in some shaving supplies. Let a parent know that you'd like to try shaving. If it's hard to talk about, say so. Try, "I'm afraid you'll say no, but I hope you will hear me out and help me decide how to handle this," or, "You may think I'm too young, but I'd like to know more about shaving." If your mom or dad says no, don't get discouraged. Ask if you can renegotiate in a few months or as the weather gets warmer.

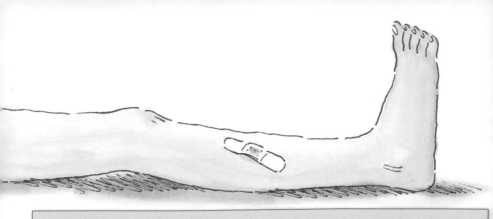

Dear American Girl,
I have a habit of picking scabs. It's really embarrassing to have scabs all over my legs. Help!
Mortified

If you keep picking your scabs, you'll have a worse problem—scars. Beat your bad habit by keeping your nails cut short and by helping scabs heal. Rub lotion onto your legs, which will make the scabs feel less tight and itchy. To prevent infection, dab antibacterial ointment directly onto the scabs. The ointment feels slippery to the touch, which may also help you keep your fingers away. Cover up your legs with pants or leggings for a week or so, just until the scabs heal. Then work to keep your legs scab-free. If you get a new scratch or cut, clean it and put on a Band-Aid right away, before temptation sets in.

Dear American Girl,
I have a wart on my knee, and it won't go away! I cover it up with Band-Aids, but when I go swimming, they fall off. Help!
Bumpy Knees

Warts are common at your age. The good news is that they sometimes go away on their own. If yours doesn't, **treat it with a product found at the drugstore,** which takes about one to two months. Can't wait that long? **See your doctor,** who might be able to get rid of the wart with a special freezing process. Until then, you can wear a waterproof Band-Aid to keep your wart under wraps while you swim. But a bandage may call more attention to your knee than the wart itself. Unless you're using a bandage that contains medicine to treat your wart, **feel free to bare your knee.** Don't feel as if you have to cover up something that's just a normal part of growing up.

Dear American Girl,
I'm not good at sports. In gym when we play kickball, I try to catch the ball. But when I fail, the kids on my team get mad at me. They also get mad when I do nothing. So what am I supposed to do?
Not a Sports Girl

It's hard to make the catch when you're worried about how your teammates will react. Tune them out by turning up the voice in your own head. **Tell yourself, "I can catch the ball. I will catch the ball. That ball's mine."** Picture yourself catching the ball, and imagine the feel of the ball in your hands. Spend time at home bouncing, kicking, and catching a ball so that ball-play starts feeling more natural. And remember that **you don't have to be a star athlete to be a good sport.** Praise other players who try hard, even when they don't succeed. Praise yourself, too, for the things you did well or improved on. If your teammates see that you're trying your best, they'll go easier on you. They'll want you around for your positive spirit, and that positive spirit will help you play better, too.

Advice from Girls

"I do gymnastics, and I'm not as advanced as everyone else. I just remind myself of how far I've come since I started. Believe that you will get better. Work hard, and you will!"
—An American Girl, age 12

Dear American Girl,
In P.E. class, they make us run every day plus do jumping jacks, sit-ups, and push-ups. During the week, I feel so sluggish. Even on the weekends, I can't get enough rest. So on Monday, I'm still as tired and sore as I was on Friday after class.
Exhausted

It sounds as if you're getting serious workouts in P.E., which can be a good thing. Just make sure you're drinking plenty of water and refueling after those workouts. Drink at least five 8-ounce glasses of water each day, and

eat a healthy snack. Stretch your muscles before and after P.E. class, focusing on the muscles you use most. If you feel rushed after class, talk to your P.E. teacher about making more time for stretching. Do some gentle stretches on the weekends, too, so that those hard-worked muscles don't stiffen up. If you're still feeling sore and tired, talk to your doctor about what else might be going on. Workouts should leave you feeling healthy and energized, not drained and sluggish.

Dear American Girl,
I have a problem. I need to get more active,
but I don't like working out.
Couch Potato

Working out shouldn't feel like work. **Focus on the fun ways you're already moving your body.** Do you dance when you hear a song you love? That counts. Do you ride your bike to go visit a friend? That counts, too. Think about ways to **add short bursts of activity throughout the day,** such as chasing your dog in the backyard, walking around the mall, or playing tag at recess. Make up a cheerleading routine with a friend, or set up an obstacle course and time each other racing through it. Do you have a video camera? Gather friends to record your own workout video. Wear crazy outfits and make up goofy routines. When you play it back, you'll work your stomach muscles—laughing! What's not to like about that?

Dear American Girl,
I'm almost 11 years old. Am I old enough to start using special exercise equipment? Or should I keep having fun for exercise?
Old Enough?

The answer is yes—and yes. You're old enough to start using some equipment, but having fun should STILL be your number-one way of getting exercise. To get aerobic exercise, which gets your heart beating faster, try racing your friends around the block. Jump rope, dance, bike, swim, play soccer, or inline skate. Treadmills and stair climbers are designed for adults, so hold off on using those. Weight-bearing exercise is also good for building strong muscles and bones. You can use light dumbbells (three to five pounds) or resistance bands, which look like huge rubber bands. To learn simple exercises, watch a DVD or have an adult teach you.

But remember that the weight of your body is enough resistance to help you build strength. Push-ups and sit-ups are great exercises and don't require any special props—just you!

Dear American Girl,
I love to sleep. When it's time to get ready for school, I just keep on sleeping. I want to get up before my mom calls me, but I can't. Can you help?
Too Tired

Are you getting enough sleep? Girls your age need about nine hours a night, sometimes more. To find out how much sleep you need, keep a diary. Every day, write down what time you wake up and what time you go to bed. Describe how you feel each morning on a scale of 1 to 5, with 1 being well-rested. If you score a 4 or 5, go to bed 15 minutes earlier that night. If you're still tired the next morning, hit the sheets 15 minutes earlier. What else can you do to help yourself rise and shine? Open the blinds or turn on the light in your room to tell your brain it's time to wake up. Set a clock radio to your favorite station so that you wake up to sounds you love. Or spend the first few minutes of every morning doing something you enjoy, such as reading a magazine or cuddling with your cat.

Dear American Girl,
I have trouble falling asleep. It usually takes
me an hour or two. What's going on?
Wide Awake

Lots of things could be keeping you up. Are you drinking soda or eating chocolate after lunchtime? Both have caffeine, which can make it hard to fall asleep. Are you exercising or playing video games too close to bedtime? Try a soothing routine instead, such as a few simple stretches, a warm bath or shower, or a good book. If you're feeling worried about something, write in your journal. Get those anxious thoughts out of your head and down on paper. Make sure your room is dark. And try going to bed at the same time every night, even on weekends. Developing a bedtime ritual will tell your body—and mind—that it's time to wind down.

Advice from Girls

"I wrap a nice, warm, fuzzy blanket around myself and read a good book with one of my cats by my side."
—An American Girl, age 10

Dear American Girl,
I get nightmares a lot, and I don't know how to control them. I'm really tired during the day from lack of sleep. Please help!
Scared to Sleep

Start by steering clear of intense TV shows or video games. Don't watch television in your bedroom before falling asleep at night. **Watch what you read, too.** Don't fill your head with scary images. If you do have a nightmare, put your overactive imagination to work to prevent another one. Close your eyes and create a funny movie or TV show in your mind. If scary images from your dream creep into the picture, **"change the channel" in your head.** Switch from scary thoughts back to something pleasant. Switch channels as many times as you need to so that you can focus on happy thoughts as you drift back to sleep.

Dear American Girl,
Every night I wake up at about 3:00, and my house makes weird noises that scare me. I wouldn't get scared if I didn't wake up in the middle of the night. Any ideas?
Nervous About Noises

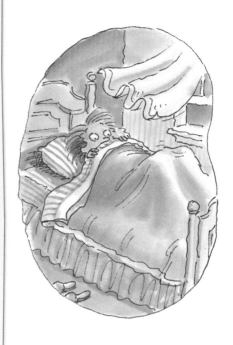

Before you go to sleep, fill your room with soothing sounds that will help drown out nighttime noises. Turn on a fan, or ask a parent if you can use a sound machine or play a CD. Keep a flashlight next to your bed so that if you do wake up, you can investigate any noises in your room. The next day, go on a hunt for the noises you heard. Shut your eyes and listen. Is that the furnace kicking in? A clock ticking? Your dog snoring? Ask a parent to help you find the source of any noises you don't recognize. You'll feel better—and sleep more soundly, too.

Dear American Girl,
I'm embarrassed to say that I still suck my thumb. Whenever I go to bed, I wake up with my thumb in my mouth. I have tried putting hot sauce on my thumb, and I also tried putting socks on my hands. Nothing works!
Hot Thumb

You'd be surprised to know how many girls struggle with the same problem. It sounds as if you've tried all the usual quick fixes. What's left? Talk to your dentist about the dangers of thumb sucking. Now that you're getting your permanent teeth, you might push your teeth out of alignment.

Ask your dentist if this is happening to your teeth, and see if he or she can make you a special retainer that will make it difficult for you to suck your thumb. By tackling this problem, you'll save yourself some embarrassment—and save your smile, too.

Dear American Girl,
I love sleepovers, but I snore. My friends always make fun of me. I try to laugh with them, but deep down it really hurts my feelings. Should I just not go to sleepovers?
Sawing Logs

Snoring may seem funny to your friends, but it can actually be unhealthy for you. You're probably not getting a good night's sleep, which can affect your mood and how well you concentrate at school. Get a check-up to find out if there is a medical reason for your snoring. Your doctor may be able to recommend some solutions, such as a mouth guard or a new sleeping position. In the meantime, keep going to sleepovers. But let your friends know what you're feeling deep down. Try, "I know you guys are just joking about my snoring, but it still hurts my feelings." If your friends want you there—and they do—they'll respect your feelings and keep their comments to themselves.

Advice from Girls

"If your friends say they're sorry, then tell them, 'Thanks for understanding how I feel. You're true friends to understand me like that.' "
—An American girl, age 12

7 Tips for Talking with Parents

(and stepparents and
aunts and grandmas
and other adults you trust)

Dear American Girl,
I'm afraid to ask my mom about puberty because I am afraid she will laugh. I get so nervous that I feel like crawling into a hole.
Hiding Out

Dear American Girl,
I don't feel comfortable talking to my dad about my body. I feel like I'm going to fall into a pit of lava if I talk to him.
Red Hot

It's normal to feel uncomfortable talking with your parents about changes that are happening to your body. But remember that every woman—including your mom and grandma—went through what you're going through now. And dads went through big changes when they were your age, too. Your dad may know more than you think he does, and what he doesn't know, he can help you find out. Your parents can almost always help you solve problems or answer questions, and you'll almost always feel better after talking with them.

1. **Plan ahead.** Don't bring something up when your parent is rushing to get out the door. Instead of asking to talk *right now,* set up a time to talk later. Ask your dad if you can go for a walk after dinner, or let your mom know that you'd like to help with dishes tonight so that the two of you can talk. If the time you suggest won't work, ask when would be a better time.

2. **Pick the right place.** Go someplace private, where other family members won't interrupt you. Turn off the TV and your cell phone. If talking face-to-face freaks you out, try talking while riding in the car or sitting side-by-side on your bed.

3. **Keep it simple.** Start with how you feel and why, such as, "I feel scared because I may get my period any day," or "I feel embarrassed because my friends wear bras and I don't." Plan your words ahead of time, and practice them in front of a mirror so that it will be easier to say them out loud.

4. **Be specific** about what you need from your parent. Advice? A shopping trip for a bra or panty liners? A big hug?

5. **Wait for a response.** Take a deep breath, and give your parent a chance to think about what you said. Use that time to congratulate yourself on getting the words out. It's not easy, but you did it.

6. **Try a new point of view.** If you don't get the response you were hoping for, try to figure out where your parents are coming from. Are they worried about you? Are they afraid you're growing up too fast? Help them to see your side of things, too. Ask, "Did you ever feel like this when you were my age?" If you and your parents disagree about whether you're ready for something, such as bras or shaving, ask if you can renegotiate in a month or two.

7. **Stay connected.** Keep the conversations going. Come up with a signal that means you need to talk, such as a ribbon tied around your bedroom doorknob or a stuffed animal perched on the kitchen counter. Or make weekly dates with your parent. If writing is easier, pass a notebook back and forth. Just keep talking. The more you do it, the easier it gets.

Break the Ice

Having trouble opening your mouth and letting the words flow? Start by asking your mom a few of these questions. Hearing about her experiences when she was your age might make it easier to talk about your own.

- Did you develop earlier, later, or about the same time as your friends?
- What did you notice first? How did you feel about it?
- When did you start wearing a bra? Who helped you buy it?
- How old were you when you got your first period? How did you tell your mom?
- What did you like about the way you looked as a girl? What didn't you like?

Isn't it a relief to know that other girls wonder and worry about the same things you do? You're not alone, and you're perfectly normal. Whatever questions you have, you can find the answers.

Be confident in your own voice, and keep talking with the people you trust. That's the best way to care for your growing body—and your spirit, too.